FOR
THE
*Love*
OF
*Binah*

FOR
THE
*Love*
OF
*Binah*

BARBARA BELLINGER

# FOR THE LOVE OF BINAH

*iUniverse books may be ordered through booksellers or by contacting:*

*iUniverse*
*1663 Liberty Drive*
*Bloomington, IN 47403*
*www.iuniverse.com*
*844-349-9409*

*ISBN: 978-1-6632-4056-9 (sc)*
*ISBN: 978-1-6632-4057-6 (e)*

*Print information available on the last page.*

*iUniverse rev. date: 05/27/2022*

I'd like to dedicate this book to my Uncle Willie Bryant, Uncle Big Boy, oldest rat in the barn and William Bryant, Uncle Plat for all the encouragement in my writings.

To the readers of this lovely story I pray that The descendants of BINAH SEE THAT THIS IS A LOOK INTO WHAT MADE THEM where they get there cooking skills from where they get there love in a relationship from why it's so deep and so strong in the mates that they choose and where they get their heroism from where they get their love of drink from their addictive personalities did they get their skills from how to make things how to design things and how most of all where they get their skills to take a little of something and make it overflowing supply...where they get there nurturing of their children and how they got their names and makes them stand out from anyone else...this story is of my vision my love fantasy of who Binah was for me...I believe she passed down to me the love that I have for my father as she had for hers then nurturing of her mother that mine was for me...how she could handle traveling and how her body was able to withstand long distances, and how she was able to adapt to her surroundings as I had to in so many situations and circumstances that played out in my life, and the talent that she had was singing dancing making your own clothes decorating whatever it was that she called home, into how she loved her man for his children even in the circumstance that they knew that it was inevitable that they could not be man and wife and how she took that love and loved whatever it was and showed it in the manner that restricted them from being whatever it was called…but most of all how she looked into the future and knew her children would be something wonderful how she knew the vision that she seen and she may never live to see it through but knowing what she gave of herself would make it happen, there's something about that word called hope helping you to realize there's something that you will never see with your own eyes but you will see it in your vision you will see it in your hope so that's why you give your best and endure the rest of whatever it takes to make that hope come true so by now I thank you for seeing me way back then thank you for all that you were because I too have hope that I may never see with my eyes but I see it with my spirit.

now fell pretty hard this year, usually a cold morning that made the wood burn in the fireplace beautiful to be home the dancing flames of the warmth that it wrong made the mornings wonderful to wake up to this morning what's a different Christmas morning was yet to come just hours away the fruit bowls were filled the general store

**Roads are not paved in Binah's day**

candy and they're stockings to fill but this morning the snow was crunching under rushing feet swiftly running to tell Binah of the Fate that are waited her young master the father of her three eldest children here come new. And surely it did come, for small but strong voice call to the knock, so who that might be come on in, at the door slightly open not to let the brisk wind enter in along with the body of the soul that came to bear the unwelcome news the sorrowful news the melancholy news that Master Morris was on his deathbed, yes, this news she was to hear, for the love in her

**Peach orchard along with many other
fruits trees well planted**

life, Sit down child what bring you in such a hurry my, ma Binah Master Morris about to leave here, and he asking for you, you need to hurry and come. Tired her bones may be but eagerly she agree, be on your way child I'll soon come, she goes to the back door and yells out for her Simon her husband and father of her children with so many years he be not her master but the one cares for her and nurtured her children and made a way to be in the comforts of what they are not many may have such a blessing but by now somehow throughout her life was blessed always be in comfort and always to have a

**This is the place where Simon young took Binah his young wife to settle down as his wife and raise a family**

blessings from song. Simon walks from the field into the back door and as she gazed upon him, by now, he knew that it was of some urgency and of news of some tragedy yet still the relief in his mind that by now may just be the time. Simon stands at the end of the stairs and looks up at her eyes I said what is it now by now Binah said it is time it is time for me to end it, may have come a little late but never worse and never coming at all I got to say farewell Simon is it all right with y'all Simon looks up at her hope in her eyes, intend to do what you got to do, you know the snow is slippery where

**Youngs Road is named after Simon young this road takes you all the way to the river**

your good shoes. And she turns to goes

back in the house shutting the door tight so

the air of the winter morning does not take

the warmth of the fire out she goes to her

room to collect her shall the one she knitted

last fall she puts on her feet the rubber boots

the one that can stand the wetness of the

snow, but she has to face the brisk of few

miles or so to carry out what it is and she

knew would soon come to goodbye the

real goodbye the real one…. When death

comes and it calls your soul this is the Great

commission that you're living story be told

as Binah wraps yourself in a shawl and looks

**This is where it all began**

in her looking Glass and sees her reflection

of how the years has taken a toll was for

some reason she sees the young girl that once

came to this land a young girl who hopes

and dreams and pickled notions of life that

she hope for and plan and little be known to

her that her life will take a turn and that are

dedication was set in a dedication of love so

the story begins.. it was a beautiful summer

when her and her mom and her paw came

in this place of wonder she was a younger

babe no more than two or three that her

mother and father took up residency in the

Norris plantation, she young Master Norris

**Many feels Gru Farmhouse fresh produce
that's sustain a community**

grew up together but he was a mere four years older than she, how they played in the fields played around the pond chasing the chickens and loving life on the farm young Master Norris from a child he was kind and generous never harsh never hitting never a rough housing but always wanting to play and giggle and laugh and enjoyed the privilege of ordering people around because he enjoy the privilege of being master of those that humor him in doing his bidding, whatever he say but then came a day, that the young master was a young man and in his eyes he saw something very beautiful

**The great trees of Camden Road**

something so delicate so loving and kind so pure and so innocent of mind, yes it was Binah, he walked with her he talked with her sharing his dreams with her, spoke of things that slave girls shouldn't have known, it was like letting her in on the big secret you know, there's so many times to his amazement she had an opinion she having an opinion she had an Outlook something that no slave black girl should know or do but to him it was marvelous to him it was something he had to love, and she had to love him too because not only did he just share, but he brought her souvenirs from his

**The Headstone of Venus firstborn William Norris**
**young but it's written in stone who his mother**
**and father is Simon and Binah Young**

travels he shared with her words in his book

he shared with her and different Outlook.

And many days they sit and say how we

wish the world were different than, their

today and you and I could be one and you

and I share the upbringing of our sons and

daughter and you and I could be you and I.

And now her mind came back to the

present she turned away from her reflection

and started herself in the direction that she

had to go and face this time at hand as her

feet treaded through the, snow she looked

around in her surroundings and over and

over and over again she knew what a magical

**Barbara's husband Rock standing in front
of the old jail house in Eutawville**

place this was, this field was once a wonderful Forest where she galloped and played with young Master Morris she can still see the tall trees that they climb and sit upon the strong branches and look down at the Earth and say wonderful and marvelous things. He shared with her what other places in the world look like shared with her how languages sound coming out of mouths of people dark and brown and white as him he brought her the souvenirs from things that would remind him of the smells of food different from what she would ever be used to. As the path transferred into the path and

**The View from the forest that the old woman told Binah
to turn around your way is clear there what a metaphor**

the road that led to the Norris House and she picked up at the trees that made an archway in the path to the house she looked at those trees and she said for those branches to touch her she has a memory of a laughter she has a memory of a joke she has a memory of a goodbye. It all started as two little children playing in the yard then as the years went on these two children were barely ever separated, young Master Norris would not eat his vegetables unless Binah was there to coach him on to finish it, and there were the times when he is having a temper tantrum because she did not want

The old jail house in Eutawville I'm quite sure a mini
spent the night in this old jail house after drinking
blackberry wine and don't forget the moonshine

to wear those short pants or the new hat that his mama would want him to wear to go to church. Then after the two grew they were often going off fishing, she teaching him how to swim, he teaching her how to skip rocks off the water. Then when young Master Morris was giving his first shotgun he was so anxious to go out into the woods with Binah and hunt rabbit, squirrel, possum, he even taught her how to shoot that rifle and it was came a competition between each other on how good they could do something how good they could skin a squirrel who could shoot that rifle and make

The old water trough in the town of Eutawville this
trough ran water constantly for many many years
until wherever the Water Source was dried out

a bullseye shoot a crow right off the branch it was sitting on…then there were those quiet times and they were either sitting way up in a tree on a strong branch just looking at the clouds naming the shapes that they made the silence was deep because the birth of a love deeper than slave and master was brewing. Yes, many things went through Binah's mind as she walked the trail to get to the Morris House. Her mind went back further as she stopped and took a rest against the tree her mind went back when she first walked this path, put her journey here that started long long ago and she was just a

**This is the Lake in Eutawville it is the swimming and fishing lake it is a Wonder to behold that in Binah's day it was just a pond and now today it is a great lake**

child, well a child meaning in the words or mind that a black slave girl would be considered a child no further than beyond the age of four, from the moment that she could hand someone something after being asked to hand that over here, that started the initiation that she had work to do. As the world around her may have seen large and so big but she really didn't understand what a small part of the world a small place that she was, to remain the rest of her life and to Bear her children here and to watch her children flourish. And that from this man she would bring about a culture that she

I can imagine Binah's feet  pressing down in the.
cool sand of the riverbank that she had visited
many many times and all of her children

would bring about a comfort that she would

bring about strong men and women with

her blood running through their veins

talented women with her gifts from the

songs that she sang from the instruments

that she played, in the quilts she made the

dresses she dawns and the braiding of hair,

after all her true origin in Africa was in her

came that hair braiding was a symbol of

royalty was a symbol of status among the

tribe in which she was always going to be a

part of, she knew back on the motherland

that prayers and the songs rang out in the

night up to the Stars about her and her fate,

**Binah's first born William Norris Young**

but like I said this is a love story not just between a man and a woman but between God and his child. God watch over her and all that she did protect her and all that she went through and abled her and everything that she did. What I can gather about my great great grandmother BINAH she arrived here on a slave ship with her parents and God shined on her from the moment she stepped on this land, Good Fortune to be filled for mother and father as they wound up at the Morris plantation. The life and the journey that it took them to get here in South Carolina was guided by Good Fortune

The Tall Pine trees that Vance and
Eutawville are known for

and good faith and the wonderful prayers
Papa could pray to God and Mama could
make a meal out anything and poppa would
start preaching to the Stars we walked a lot
we walked a whole lot but that's what legs
are for Papa would say, and God bless us in
so many ways and we came upon a
campground or shanty town or just a
settlement there was something always there
for our hands to do, when it came to mama
cooking she could put a wash pot together
and make everybody feel good and when
everybody was feeling good everybody sang
and then when they sang then somebody

**The first thing to be established in
Eutawville and Vance is the railroad**

will preach the good word and then Papa
would forcefully bring out like a roaring
lion saying, God has got his plan for us,
Grandma Binah was always in something
nice and lace she liked hand ordering it said
she had the fastest hands on this side of
Eutawville that can make a lace collar or
embroider something real pretty for
someone. I guess when it was finally
understood and truly believed that the
slavery time has ended everybody's Free.
Said they are going to do something call
with this thing called reconstruction and so
make sure that all the Black people were

Barbara and her husband Michael but
he's better known as Rock

going to get something Fair to help them get along to build their own life on their own farms well that's what they say now, now I would not like my daddy said I would not put my neck on the chopping block and guarantee that now that is what I heard they say now I will not put my neck on the chopping block to make it so now. Binah stops and rest a minute contemplate Lord I should have brought some water or a biscuit I need this morning but lo and behold one of her grand running down the path with a lunch bucket nice cold water some cornbread and some biscuits. Seems like children these

**Barbara and her husband Michael**

days got some good minds, here grandma I
thought you might need something you did
not have a breakfast this morning with us
and that is a long walk you getting ready to
take want me to walk a little way with you
grandma, no time you going back and finish
up what you got to do and head on out to
school I will see you later. Binah takes the
lunch box and looks inside and sure enough
this child done pack a good lunch enough
where I can have something for my strength
going and, on my strength, coming back
lordly bless his little heart. As Binah
approaches the thick wooded area her heart

**The tree canopy covered roads are some of the
great wonders in Eutawville and Vance**

races in the thought that she might see her

old friend, Miss Mookie the woman who

lives in the woods, all her life Miss Monike

that is always shown up in her days of days

and her time in time….. surely her first

meeting Miss Mookie happened when she

was a child just arriving to this place to this

place and she'll always be and another good

morning breeze was cool Binah knew she

had to make her way closest to the edge of

the woods as soon as she could, for the sun

heat would make it difficult to walk in this

open plane of the field, she talked to her

God saying hymns of love to him as he

strengthened her on this journey. The sweet smell of wild onions and sassafras roots cleared her mind all the things that she was about to give away, it had been some years since she seen Master Norris, for he and she were getting up in age now and the world was such a different place now than when they first met, but she was just a mere child the same as young Master Norris, she remembers the excitement that she had in her young mind when she jumped down off the wagon of her mom and dad when they arrived on the Norris plantation, the long journey that it took to get there and the surprising element of where they were going and what was waiting for their arrival but Papa put such a mystery behind the journey, and mama was so calm and not asking Papa what's to become of us in this place that he's so assumingly packed up all that we owned all that we had. Papa being so sure that this journey at its end will be a good thing... Binah still can feel the excitement, of such a grand place on the arrival everything seems like something out of a story book out of a story she's heard old women spoke of in their journeys as they set on campfires in exchange news and exchanged information and exchange experience always shared so one could know what one is walking into, all the pitfalls that are any negro traveling may have been so that negroes were free but they weren't free from the dangers of the folks that didn't agree. Her papa had scars of such brutality and her mama too, that was long before she was born, Papa scars may have been deep but the deep scars Mama wore from the children she couldn't keep, I guess that's why they love Binah so much because she was the only child that her mama could keep, and the old woman in the woods told Binah of the many secrets that just couldn't keep, as the breeze blew

across Binah's face the recollection and then

warmth of summer day long gone, and the

times she looked at her reflection in the

pond, she remembers the cool water she

drank behind her she saw an image that

didn't frighten her but made her stand still

to make sure that it wasn't phantom spirit

or it's just a shadow of a tree, no it was the

old woman in the woods, as Binah slowly

turned and leaning back on our arms and

said to her who be you, and the old woman

questioned her right back saying no my

child who will be you, do you know who

you are? And Binah being such an inquisitive child, questioned her right back, well who do you think I might be? The old woman looked into her eyes, and says I know who you be, you are the one I wait for, I have wait for you a long time, I have wait for you because the road had to lead you here, because you the one, you the one that have to bring them all here, yes, you are the one they all must come from, that they are to be hundreds of them…. Yes, my child you are the one, the one that is carrying the seeds, bare all of them that is going to come and make this land a good land, all them souls

that need to come to this earth will come
and be good people I will share the love of
God, I make this place where spirit of God
will dwell yes you child right now that is all
I can tell…. Now you go and be a good girl
and do as your told and be kind, be kind to
the young Master Morris, from that day on,
throughout Binah's life the old woman
would show up in all her days of days and
time in time. And every time she see the
old woman, her appearance never changed,
a white silk hair intertwine in a rag that she
wore on her head her rubber face which
sharp lines and her grayish blue eyes that

look like marbles her big bosom that hung

low, and it always seems like she had on two

or three sets of clothes, her skirt drag the

ground in her hand that held on to a large

branch that she used for walking stick was

just as leathery looking, and topped off with

her long yellowish fingernails, it was evident

that she did a lot of work with her hands,

her cloths showed evidence of stains that she

was not idle……….. and truly as the old

woman had told Binah, they became close

companion and friend to young Master

Norris. There was plenty to do around the

Norris plantation and plenty of hands plenty

of work day in and day out always building always planting, every season of the year there was always something they had to do in a hurry so much of it and so far to go for it to be sold and being divided among many people coming and going, then there were the Days that fun and laughter music and dancing, yes the negroes had their way of celebrating their day of days celebrating the seasons in and out celebrating when the crops were done and all was done on time, yes God showed favor in this land, yes and there was a Love in this Land, every time you look around somebody was getting hitched and every time you look round a baby was being born, yes you see when the body is not being too badly worn out, and you can give time to worship God and time to sweep your own floors, time to make your own rooms and the roof don't leak in the cold winds of Winter is shut out Cuz your shelters nice and tightly built with good worked wood and your house is packed nice and tight with a nice hard my mire clay, and each cotton season there's enough spare cotton to make nice soft beds, and the natural talent that the women folk have mastered the art of the most beautiful patch

quilt spreads that keeps you warm and toasty,
when there's a potbelly stove in every cabin
a nice heavy iron to press off cloth, to where
it's understood the term Sunday best truly
meant better than all the rest of what you
wear in the ordinary day. Even though times
have changed so very much since Binah's
youthful memories she still says that the
days of her youth were much better than the
days of our old age who to think hard
working as people were known to do could
live past the age of 70 not even the thinking
to be 92, but here she is tracing back from
now till then. I understand she have come

to her fork in the road, Binah stops to take

a bite of a biscuit, the song comes across her

lips and she hums and chews. Stand by me

Lord stands by me when My Friends do not

understand, stand by me, when have done

the best, I can stand by me….. yesterday had

gone and came upon the moment when her

heart was full of love, but it was the kind of

love at all could not understand or want to

understand you see it was commonplace for

the master that any of the Masters son would

take a liking to the thick and voluptuous

young slave girls that they owned on any

given plantation, but this was not that kind

of time you see slaves were free but Binah was not free to love who she wanted to. I said years went by and separation became evident that each man held his own, his own land, his on house, his own children, his own wife, even though all that freedom was, there were still the ties that bind. It was still things set in place that separate, there were things that love could not withstand no matter how hard the love was. And then It came upon Binah, young Master Morris very very early but not very very sudden, the feeling stirred up in them every time they were alone either fishing at the pond or walking back from the cow pasture, moments of weakness came upon them every time a thickness in the air, the old woman in the woods didn't have to tell Binah of what she was feeling, nor young Master Norris for they seen it all around them they seen love they seen affection it seemed courtships and they seem when it was to be smitten by one..........., and that day finally came upon them when it had to happen, when it was bound to happen........ the passion was so hard and heavy that it overcame them and before they could even ration it or make sense of it, it was done.

And truly a love was born that day, a love that only heaven could protect, the young Master Norris did with it only a young Master could do, run and leave Binah there, left to pull her thoughts together but as time and time would be the old woman showed up and comforting her telling her it has begun. Binah said the words she knew the answers to, what has begun old woman what? The door, the door you came to open, to let those beautiful souls from heaven come in to this world, this world that needs them so much, yes child, it has begun, the glow is already on you, it'll be easier from here, the first three souls will be from here and they will go in three parts of the world and they will grow from there, but then the hard part will come when the master will have to do what he has to do, because what you and he have for one another will never be, for while in your tender youth you let these three souls come through you and they will have what it takes to have what this land need to bring the love of God on this place and let it stay for a time of time till that number will grow, they will spread all over this world Cuz that's what the Lord sent us here for to make this world full of his love that he can dwell here, so we put

our hands to the gospel plow and thy will

be done on Earth as it is in heaven till his

kingdom come..... truly how does one

know what is in a young girl's mind or even

in her parents to know their young child is

with child and the father of that child is the

hand that feeds them, having to accept what

was the norm in those days of a young

master taking unto himself what one would

say belongs to him in their ignorance they

cannot see it or accept it in any other way,

there is no rejoicing or gladness that these

two have come together and a possible

Union could be how preposterous that would be. Now the young master must put on a façade of yes, he indulges in that which was looked upon to be his God-given right, and more or less to say that the young woman is best to look that as a prize cow. Never would either of their parents choose to realize or even conceive that these two were in love with one another any other rational thinking on anybody's part would not be heard or conceived of to be anything other than what the law of the land say it is, after months roll by and the anticipation Like I said Mama and Papa loved their child

Binah

so they handled her with kid gloves, because

everybody know what has befallen their

child but in an odd way there was no shame

you know, no just another black girl carrying

the Master's child, it did bother them

somehow his attention to her and her well-

being, refusing to let her work in the fields

around the yard and brought her into the

house when she did light things, like polish

the silverware wash the dishes fold the linen

make beds empty chamber pots sewing and

mending knitting and crocheting tedious

needlework on lace and linens….. and to

this credited her skills she had all the time

*Barbara Bellinger*

truly impressed by Morris household, what manners and courteousness that this child had about herself, like her mama always told her good manners will take you where money can't, in the Norris house he was able to hear books being read she was able to hear words being said she was able to take in like a sponge all things a good manners and then some and all that she saw them do she mimicked quite well and made her a credit to her race to be so well reared and when that final day had come for this child to be born the anticipation was high oh it was buzzed all around the land about Binah was about to give birth. Master Norris had two midwives come Cuz just like how he anticipated that this was going to be a long one 12 hours it took but surely it came bouncing bright light damn nah white baby boy with long brownish hair, and strong lungs you can hear him holler all through the woods down near the meeting tree, young Master Norris ran to her mom and Pa and told of their grandchild and what a beautiful baby boy by the time it got all the way around you would think that she gave birth to albino but when everybody kept putting emphasis on how light and bright he was…. Yes, young Master Norris was a proud papa just saying that his jeans were stronger than a negro. but was it? And finally look down at the little child she could hear the old woman's voice, she looked at her little son's face seen the blurred lines between race and she understood what the old woman meant that he would come equipped with what he needs to make it in this world…….

Now back in those days when the son is born and it is the first born oh that was a time of celebration that was a time of butchering a hog, and cooking all the good fixing and music and foot stomping and plenty of singing….. the beautiful thing about this young boy's birth was the time that the world was set in, it was a time of the great separation, some call it the reconstruction some call it 40 acres (about twice the area of Chicago's Millennium Park) and a mule some call it getting their comeuppance no matter what it was called it was still time when things were taking shape, where he will have a place in this world, it will make difference in so many lives yet to come, yes the child and she named him William. William grew to a wonderful beautiful little boy so beautiful that his Papa didn't mind being seen with him and Binah had become so well versed in what was required of being in the Master's house, taking care of the Norris family and she was now a permanent fixture there, as her parents had moved on into their own piece of land and started their own farming and sharecropping.

It wasn't for long that Binah was now about to have his second child, and yet again Binah gave birth to a Norris second son that she mean Daniel and he too was born light bright damn near White, the Master had two sons now to look upon and show his love and kindness without having too much harsh

and ridicule from his white community or
his family of stature, you see these two boys
grew to enjoyed the privileges that children of
their circumstances usually have, things were
getting quite obvious to the Norris family
that this was something more than what God
fear and white folks will tolerate…. And so as
the old woman in the woods warned Binah
about, and at times final couldn't accept her
fate or the reality of what was happening
she gave birth to a third child and this time
beautiful baby girl that she named Ida,
a dreadful decision was made and had to
come, but old woman in the woods warned

her of it and told her not to tangle her heart into thinking that it could be something other than and surely as the day brings upon the sunshine and the night brings upon the Moon the Norris family gave Young Master Morris the command to put Binah in her place, it has now become intolerable and it was becoming quite evident that it was more than a master and slave relationship it had been obviously a full-blown love affair and that was not to be tolerated in no way shape form or fashion.

Young Norris have some decisions to make and he thought of a good one, he took it upon himself to find a negro that

was binding to one of his fellow former

slave owners to hand Binah over to as a

wife, for such as time as those were if he

did not succumb to his family's wishes

didn't abide by the law of the land Binah

and her children would have been killed

and as she ran in the woods looking for

the old woman The Old woman made her

wait three days until her heart just couldn't

stand no mor, she screamed out and called

for God's mercy.....

And surely the old woman came and

gave her words of console, the man that

your master gives you to, you be kind and beautiful and God will truly bless you and you will be fruitful and multiply because the door is open child through you and they have to come and they will come and they will be many everything that you are, they will have a little bit of you and everything that makes them great will have the bit of him in them too, but the greatest thing that they will have and that they will be, are the souls that God send to this world to make this world good enough for God to bring his kingdom, when you were a soul in heaven and God sent his counselor of angels to you and asked you would you be a willing soul to come and be the one to let the door open so the soul of God can come and make this lower part of heaven a place where he can dwell in and you that soul said yes Lord send me and so he did and so you are, do not let your flesh take control of what your soul is here to do the soul is so willing but the flesh is weak, remember that child remember that. Well for the days will come, will you, will cry over your children and all this land but because you the one who opened the door. God will be there for you always he will supply all your needs, He will be there for every tear that fall and for every morsel you eat and for every time you sleep, He will give you dreams and give you visions and you will see the love of God grows strong like a tree, so hush child everything's all right, you go now, you go and stay in the light....

And surely like the old woman said Master Morris gave Binah to Simon Young to be wed...

You know there's always a twist of fate that happens when a woman is obedient to the will of God and love will show itself in all its truest form, Binah was more blessed with love then she thought she knew what

love was and what love felt like was Simon

Young it was strong, what they call back

then strong Young Buck, when she put all

her belongings in his wagon and her children

and seen the sight of the Norris plantation

fade away in the dust cloud of the road not to

be seen again for quite a long time, she sat on

that wagon seat next to the strong beautiful

black man, who had a gentle voice warm eyes

and when he pulled into the yard and looked

at the strong well-built cabin she looked at

him again with different eyes, she said who

help you do all this and he said with a strong

but proud voice I did all this here myself and the help of some brotherly love, we folks over here on this side of the pond we looked out for one another, it was as if the scales fell from her eyes and she looked around at her surroundings on the ride she looked at her surroundings and saw a community, she saw a community of black people with their own houses with their own yards with their own fields and their own Wells and their own outhouses yes it was a different world and she was still young enough to make a difference in her life, she was still young enough and vibrant enough to enjoy freedom.

Simon Young did more than take Binah

off Master Morris hands he opened her eyes

to what life truly can be when you love

someone, when you are devoted to someone,

when you become part of something much

bigger than yourself, when you can see the

big picture from another perspective and

this made her happy..... Binah was able

to reconnect with her mother and father

and to now see what did become of some

of her childhood friends that before she

was embedded into the Norris household

she had but all isolated herself with her

children and the housekeeping of the

Norris family, even though it was just a few years in the separation of the people that she was acquainted with and familiar with, but time was moving so fast and the world was changing swiftly along with it, her people had moved forward in leaps and bounds and all to her amazement she was so welcomed... ... ..

In the Cool breeze of the evening she sit on the front porch after she put her children to bed and she watch Simon like his pipe and the sweet tobacco smell filled the air she looks across the plane and see nothing there, she said to Simon, how did all this come about so fast and Simon simply said

all the years we've been building houses and

making home for white folks it was nothing

but a hop skip and a jump for us to make our

own and we show working hard together

to keep it that way and make it better for

our children yet to come. Binah looked at

Simon and said can I tell you something and

you won't think me crazy, Simon looks at

her and said woman nothing you can say

that can make me think you crazy, she said

Simon someone told me that I opened the

door, they told me that I opened the door

for The souls of heaven to come down here

to the lowest part of heaven to make it for

the Lord can dwell in this world, Simon

gently says to her there's so much that you

won't believe that is yet to come all these

things that making us work hard at making

a living, somebody going to come and make

it easy, while we sitting over here on this

porch somewhere on the other side of this

whole big world is a war, people fighting

killing one another over land over having

power over another man, all these things

that we hear about happening way on the

other side of the world and some just a

couple of hundred miles from here, we here

in this place living in peace and we have to do the will of God if we want to stay in peace…. Simon spoke some other words to her that made her heart anchor into his love he said woman I see how you love them three children of yours, but when the Lord give us children I want you to love them even harder, Cuz they won't have what do your three children have, their light skin it's going to take them a little further and our little black children won't have half a chance, we going to love them and bring them up in a godly way, I tell you woman the world that's coming our children and their children are going to be the ones to enjoy what true freedom look like, and they might not have it all totally then they still will have a fight but the fight begins here the training begins here the discipline begin here,

You got to teach them what hard work looks like, we got to teach them what come up out the ground, we got to teach them what they can make with their hands, we got to teach them how to bring what they dream about to the forefront and make it happen, but none of it will happen without God... Some of them might be bad apples but that's to be expected in all form of life, a frog may have two heads a dog may have two tails, whenever one of God's creations do with them meant to do, only man got the choice to do good or do bad, but they learn to make them choice because of the ones who bring them in this life, the one who teach you one who love them or the one who hurts them…. And I do declare sometimes I believe that the Lord let the bad seeds sprout just to remind us that man is not perfect yet, only when his kingdom come will that be so and it isn't coming so till we learn how to love thy neighbor, it is what you doing the others that you have

others doing to you that is what the good

book says anyway... ...

Binah so amazingly look at Simon, says

good book, you got a good book, man you

tell me you can read, Simon smile with

another ability to impress Binah, yes, I can

read it a little bit enough to get me by, that

I'm not cheated when I go to sell my crops.

I know enough for any papers I have to sign

or need in order to keep my land and we

have a good book lessons from the preacher

that come through here, and I can sign my

name, Simon goes in his pocket and pulls

out a piece of paper and shows Binah, see this paper this paper says that this property belong to me how many acres I got and when I got it and it's paid in full, see here that's the magistrate stamps and right there, that's is my signature... ...

See when that censors man come around counting who all lives here. I can say who we are and sign our names right on that censor's paper.... now ain't God good, and Binah replies yes Simon yes sir God is good....all the time.

Here is where it started from, I believe the knack the we have always made sure that we have a plan with our mates, and where it goes wrong is when one of us stray away from the plans that carries all are hopes and dreams on to make a family. Then as time went on and just like that conversation that Binah and Simon had on that porch way back then, it came true like a bolt of lightning, their children was born, and their children was born, the censor's man did come and yes Simon wrote all their names and ages with his own hand...

Now here right here is where I Barbara, shall stop on my speculation on who did what and naming names and so fourth and

so on, this not what this book is about, we
all know the story that we all was told to
us on our family reunion program yes, the
one that goes something like this... willie
Williams 1789-6/05/1869 and his wife Bina
Williams gave birth to our beloved Binah
1852 09/26/1934 while working as slaves
on the Norris plantation.

Our beloved Binah worked in the main
house and being a beautiful full figured young
lady, she caught the eye of Master George
Manley Norris.3/27/1848-12/24/1934

Even after the emancipation proclamation
Binah continued to work in the plantation

Masters house, where she bore three children for the young Master their names where William, Daniel, and Ida.

This Norris house still stands today on Camden Rd. in the Vance, S.C. community

Binah married Simon young 1878 to this union six children were born Tode, Callie, Lymas, Joseph, Duks and Christine...and that is the story and we are sticking to it.

So, the story that you are reading in this book is all my love and dreams of Binah.

There is no way, can I believe that my children and the people I call family could not have come into this universe of ours without there being a love so wide that it has span into six generations, of the most talented, power filled, dotting mothers, discipline caring fathers, any sport you name it, musicians, songbirds, overcomers, leaders, community builders, activist, long distance runners, educator, woke group of people you will ever meet. Hats what's been told and that story I'm sticking to it.....

So the story ends that if you do the math, Binah does live to a ripe old age and here is where I thank her, I thank her for taking that long walk to say good bye to the man that once embodied a sprit that could be loved and did give love, and I thank her for not fighting the path that she had to take to ensure the safe passage of my birth, for giving me the answers of all my why?, The wonderful knowing of why not...And forever exhale phase. Oh, I see now!

And understanding of why true love came to me so late in life, I am so thankful for my beautiful husband Michael the one man that gave me that Simon kind of love and life, like GGGBinah I came into our marriage with my children and nurtured and love his children like they were my own children.....

When I sit at my dressing table and look in the

mirror, I can see my likeness of GGGBinah, at family gatherings I can see GGGBinah in the way on my turn the head and her her in the laughter, taste her cooking in that plate of hop-n-john, and the got no problem taking trip to get to where ever we say we going to meet up at, Road worriers...............

This story of mine has to end with me telling all all I know,

All I know is that before my birth I was soul in Hevan in heaven doing whatever it is that you do in haven but one Heverly Counceller of came and asked me a question and the question was

Would you go?? And me being a soul in heaven I said yes Lord send me.......

So, there I was in my mother's womb I looked around and said where are my mother and father aright then my personal relationship began with God hey Tho I walk through the valley of death I will fear on evil for Tho art with...............me

And being on this earth for the many years that I have been I am so pleased to know that mission is not done yet we still have so much to, we have let this world know and understands He has so much more life for you, make the world know that God is Love and until the hold world knows it his kingdom won't come down.... God is Holy he cannot dwell there is sin, that's why He had to turn his face when Jesus was on the cross because Jesus placed all our sins on himself, Oh Thank you Lord, thank you.......

As Binah had hoped the old lady was there, she looked Binah up and down, and says, you did fine for yourself, I am proud of you child you are proof that being obedience to God is possible.

Now I know where you going, but there is nothing there for you child, Binah reply

I know I am just going to show my respect,

The old woman graped Binah by the hand

and said it is finished my sweet child, there

is no gleam in his eyes for you he will not

hear your voice and have a truth awaking,

that his true love holds his hand and bits

him farewell on his journey to his Heaven,

No dear one, you see before you the

truth of what I say to you, look look, do

you see what hinders your journey ahead,

you see the woods here all growed up, you

see the stick-a-burrs all on the bottom of

your cloths, look at all them vines ready to

cut your skin, turn around and look back

where you just came from, you see how

everywhere is clear. Look back and go back

to where all the love and heard word paid

off, yes it paid off for you Binah, that little

boy that brought you that lunch bucket, will

be the one that will feed The Lords sheep

and that first born of yall own, has been

done right by his father if you must know,

He ant tell you because so long as there are

no worries about being secure in what you

have, and he is a great man three hundred

acres he holds the deed to, and has enough

children to work it and their children and

their children will live on it and enjoy the

fruit of their labor.............Binah reached out her hand to find a strong tree branch to lean on as the tears fell from her eyes and she put her face in her hands and screamed into them, LORD HELP ME PLEASE.... when Binah looked the old woman was gone...And with a soft whisper Binah says thank you Lord for you have surely supplied all my needs...Binah picks of some of the stick-a-burrs and held them in her hand and felt the sharp peck's and says such a small thing that can hurt so bad, she threw them to the ground and gave heard snuff and a sharp spit on them, and a deep inhale and felt the warmth of the sun on her face and headed back the way she came. And just as the old woman, opened her eyes to the truth when she returned and looked around, there it was her own paradise, everything grew here, pecan trees. Peach trees, corn fields, sweet potatoes, white potatoes, fine livestock, hogs big as ponies, some of the best grape wine, good enough for communion, and the corn made the best white lighting that would have you curled up like a baby, and the mildest smoking tobacco with the sweetest aroma, that made ending the day with corncob pipe stuff with it a best a man or woman can get ... So that's my story and I'm sticking to it. Again, I thank my Great Great Great-grandmother Binah for the eighty-two years she spent on this side of heaven, for being the Gate, for I will enter His Gate with Joy and Thanksgiving....

Binah may have never wear the name Norris, so she named her first born William Norris Young and throughout the generations the name William is the name of a son....

The end

Printed in the United States
by Baker & Taylor Publisher Services